JOURNEY OF

Love

Also from the Boys Town Press

For Parents

Common Sense Parenting®
Common Sense Parenting of Toddlers and Preschoolers
Common Sense Parenting Learn-at-Home Video Kit
Angry Kids, Frustrated Parents
Parenting to Build Character in Your Teen
Dealing with Your Kids' 7 Biggest Troubles
Parents and Kids Talking about School Violence
Practical Tools for Foster Parents

For Adolescents

A Good Friend
Who's in the Mirror?
What's Right for Me?
Boundaries: A Guide for Teens

For Professionals

Teaching Social Skills to Youth
Safe and Effective Secondary Schools
The Well-Managed Classroom
The Well-Managed Classroom for Catholic Schools
The Ongoing Journey
Dangerous Kids
Building Skills in High-Risk Families

For a free Boys Town Press catalog, call
1-800-282-6657. www.girlsandboystown.org/btpress

Teens and parents who need help with any problem
can call the Girls and Boys Town National Hotline at
1-800-448-3000 anytime.

JOURNEY OF
Love

READER

Essays to Help Teens Find God's Purpose for Relationships

VAL J. PETER

BOYS
TOWN
PRESS

BOYS TOWN, NEBRASKA

Journey of Love Reader

Published by the Boys Town Press
Boys Town, Nebraska 68010

© 2001 Father Flanagan's Boys' Home

ISBN 1-889322-48-2

www.girlsandboystown.org/btpress

The Boys Town Press is the publishing division of Girls and Boys Town, the original Father Flanagan's Boys' Home.

Publisher's Cataloging-in-Publication
(Provided by Quality Books, Inc.)

Peter, Val J.
  Journey of love reader / by Val J. Peter -- 1st ed.
  p. cm.
  ISBN: 1-889322-48-2

  1. Christian education--Textbooks for teenagers.
2. Teenagers--Religious life. 3. Man-woman relationships--
Religious aspect--Christianity. 4. Spirituality.
5. Love--Religious aspects--Christianity.   I. Title.

BV1485.P48 2001   268'.433
                             QBI01-200254

10   9   8   7   6   5   4   3   2   1

Table of Contents

Breaking Up Is Hard to Do

Everyone knows that the cartoons which millions of kids watch on television, especially on Saturday mornings, are not real. They're cartoons. "They're Hollywood." To say something is "Hollywood" means it's unreal. It doesn't really happen. It's make believe. It's artificial, plastic. It exists in the imagination.

And while all of us know that cartoons are "Hollywood," unfortunately, many of us do not realize that the boy-girl relationships as seen on TV and in the movies are unreal, too. They are artificial.

What's unreal about the boy-girl relationships we see in movies? Let me give you some examples:

- Just to appear in a short scene for one or two minutes, an actress may take two to three hours or more for makeup. That's unreal. Nobody does that in real life.

- If a girl did, she would spend all of her time getting ready and not much time "being seen."

- The clothes all come from "wardrobe." The actors don't have to pay for them. The clothes are not chosen to be practical. And they're awfully expensive.

- Movies often portray boy-girl relationships as getting into bed or getting out of bed or getting ready to get into bed or out of bed. That's unreal, too. That's not what happens in real life, or if it does, it's a tragedy.

- The biggest "Hollywood" part of TV and movies is the idea that kids are happy doing all of this, when in reality, it only leads to bitter unhappiness. I've never seen a situation where sex between a high school boy and a high school girl didn't mean one or both of them getting hurt. Inflicting pain and hurt on people doesn't sound like happiness.

So what are some realistic ideas about boy-girl relationships in high school?

1. The first thing to remember is their purpose. The purpose of all high school relationships, including boy-girl relationships, should be friendship, friendship, friendship.

   Hollywood says the purpose is drugs, sex, and rock and roll. That's Hollywood; it's fantasy. Perhaps it's fun to watch in a movie. But it leads to unhappiness if you practice it in real life now (and in the life to come).

2. Almost all relationships in high school break up or go away. They do not last forever. Most do not even last a year beyond high school. it's not bad, that's just the way things are. And that's why it's always good to have more than one friend. It's good to have many friends as you go through high school. Expect that you will have fun with the people you are friends with in high school, but you will most likely not spend your life with them.

   Hollywood sometimes wants us to think "only of today" not tomorrow or into the future. That too is fantasy. That's not realistic. Realistically, you have a future, not just a present. We need to realize that breaking up in a high school relationship is bound to happen, and we all know it is hard to do.

3. The first rule for success is not to build your life and dreams around high school relationships or around one other person. You need to have other friends. Don't drop them. You need to do things with your friends. And you need to keep doing the fun things you did before a relationship started.

   Hollywood sometimes says you drop all other relationships and build your world around one person. That's fantasy – harmful and hurtful.

4. Keep your life and dreams in high school as big and as full of potential as possible. Please don't plan for your

future with a mind that two of you will be together always. Do not plan your future by asking what would be best for you together. Do not plan your future as if the other person will even be present.

Hollywood oftentimes tells stories about kids who build their whole future around the other person and expect always to be together. And then the story ends tragically, sometimes even in death. It makes a great movie. And you can cry in the theater. But you surely wouldn't want those kinds of things to happen to you.

5. Be honest about your feelings for the other person. In high school relationships there are often feelings that make you uncomfortable about the other person. This is especially true when they ask you to do things you don't want to for them. Especially when they ask you to act differently than you did before. When they ask you to not spend time with your old friends. When they ask you to do sexual things "if you want to keep the friendship." "Have sex with me or I'll kill myself." Address your feelings right away. If necessary, break off the relationship.

When a friendship ends, we feel bad enough anyway. We'll feel doubly bad if we did not pay attention to those uncomfortable feelings and did things that we are now ashamed of ourselves for doing.

6. For your own good health, your emotional health, your spiritual health, your physical health, avoid sex. It will not make things better.

Sex has two purposes and they both begin with a "b": bonding and babies. Bonding means that whether you want it or not, sex makes it hard to walk away from a relationship. This is especially true for the girl. It is not sexist to say that. In our culture, girls think much more in terms of relationships than boys do. Girls, for example, tend to think of how much they put into a relationship and they expect boys to put in an equal amount.

Boys don't think that way. They tend to think of what other boys put into relationships (not an equal amount!) or what their father put into the relationship with their mother. So high school boys do not think they should put as much into the relationship as the girl, but only as much as other boys do or their father did. That means putting very little into a relationship. That's got to be frustrating to a girl. And then you put the psychological bonding of sex on top of it, and it simply makes things much more painful and much more complicated.

Why does sex mean bonding and babies? Because that is the way God, the Creator, made it. That is the purpose of it. Sex is meant for marriage and children. It helps bond husband and wife together. Any use of it outside of marriage only hurts people. After all, what high school girl wants bonding with a boy who only uses her and then walks away when he gets bored or gets fearful of a "real relationship"?

There are several conclusions and they are clear:

- The more a relationship is a friendship, the healthier it will be, both when you are in a relationship and when it breaks up.

- The more a relationship involves bonding, the more your heart will be broken. And the more it will feel like a divorce when the relationship ends.

REFLECTION QUESTIONS

Directions: After reading Chapter 1, answer the following questions.

1. What does it mean to say something is 'Hollywood"?

2. Name three things that are unreal about the boy-girl relationships we see in the movies.

3. What is the true purpose of high school boy-girl relationships?

4. Why is it wrong to build your life and dreams around a high school relationship?

5. What are the two purposes of sex?

   B_____

   B_____

6. Explain how boys and girls think differently about sex and relationships.

7. Explain the two conclusions given at the end of the chapter.

2

Wherever You Go, I Will Go

"I dare you to jump across that puddle." "I dare you to walk on that ledge." "I dare you to climb that fence."

How often did we hear these words when we were very, very young, spoken by other kids ages four, five, and six? When we were that age, we quickly learned not to pay any attention to such dares. It was all a game. We didn't lose any friends by saying no. We did not make any enemies. We did not lose face. We did not consider it important enough to feel bad about. It was just all part of the teasing of childhood. Oh, I suppose some kids got intimidated, but not many.

And that's why it seems so strange that when we are adolescents we get intimidated by similar language. Let's look at it for a minute.

What would you do if someone in your group pulled out a plastic bag of pills and started passing them around? Would you accept the dare?

What would you do if you walked into a room and your buddies were passing a joint around? Would you accept the dare?

What if your boyfriend or girlfriend said, "It's time to get down." Would you accept the dare?

What if a friend dared you to take a CD from a store? Would you accept the dare?

Why is it so much harder when we are adolescents to say "no" than it is when we are children?

First note that it is only for about ten to fifteen years of our lives (years called adolescence) that we go through a period where it is very difficult to say "no" to a dare. Later on, it will be just as easy to say "no" to dares as when we were children. That information in itself helps some kids put these adolescent dares in a proper perspective. It's not like it's going to last forever – only a few years.

Secondly, there are some dares that we should say "yes" to when we are adolescents. The Lord is going to say: "I dare you to stand up for what you know is right." That's a dare we ought to accept. Why?

Because the Lord only dares us to do good things, not bad. The Lord dared us when we were four or five to trust when we were afraid of the dark. We learned not to be afraid. We learned to trust the Lord.

And when we are older and married and a parent and we are dared to "fool around a little bit," it is easier for us to say "no." It's easier for us to trust the Lord. We have so much to lose. We have so much love, caring, and sharing with our children and with our spouse. Who wants to throw that away?

There is the key insight right there. When we are adolescents, we don't see ourselves as having as much security, loving, caring, and sharing in our family as we experienced when we were very small children. Relationships in the adolescent years seem so tenuous. We seem so much in need with so little assurance that these needs will be met. We want so much to be accepted and loved. We don't feel as much love and acceptance. That's why it's so hard in adolescence to say "no" to the dares.

The degree to which you keep yourself close to the Lord is the degree to which you will have strong enough feelings of love and security to be able to say "no" to the dares. The degree to which you feel enough caring and sharing in relationships with your friends who dare you to do good things, is the degree to which you can say "no" to the dares for bad things. The degree to which you feel loved and secure in your relationship with your mom or dad is the degree to which you can dare to be different.

A lot of people talk about "the need for adolescents to clarify their values." Think of it this way. As a child you knew what your values were – no lying, cheating, stealing, drugs, sex, alcohol – to the degree you felt loved and secure in your family. Those values have not changed. They are as true in adolescence as they were in your childhood.

Do not let someone talk you into betraying these values. That would be self-betrayal. Be an adolescent of moral courage. You just need to get in touch with enough love and acceptance to live those values out. By doing so, you'll feel good about yourself, good about your relationships, and good about life.

REFLECTION QUESTIONS

Directions: After reading Chapter 2, answer the following questions.

1. Why is it harder to say "no" to our friends' dares when we are adolescents than when we are children?

2. Explain the kinds of dares we should say "yes" to.

3. What can help you be strong enough to say "no" to dares?

Friends Are Forever

We are all emotionally hurt at times. This kind of hurt isn't like a headache. You can take an aspirin for a headache and it goes away. The hurt isn't like a broken bone. You can have the bone set, and it heals. Emotional hurt is in the heart. There are three "medications" for it.

The first is to be by yourself for a while. Suppose someone you trusted spread lies about you. It really hurts. You need to take time by yourself. Do a little mourning. You need quiet time to let the feeling of sorrow say the important things it has to say to your heart. There are tears, too. Tears that well up inside, tears for the hopes that were washed away.

There is a beginning, a middle, and an end to the loneliness. Don't make it too short; don't make it too long. Don't make it too fast; don't make it too slow. Like a rain-filled sky, the rains will stop when the clouds are empty.

The second thing that you need most importantly for emotional hurts is a true and trusted friend. A friend is one to be there for you when you are down – to pick you up. A friend is there to listen to you – not just to give advice. A friend is there "to care for you through laughter and through tears."

When the loneliness is done, you need to talk to a friend, to share the pain, to dry your tears. That's why "friends are forever."

Poetry and music are filled with the praise of friends. "If we hold on together, I know our dreams will never die." And an old favorite: "You can count on me. I'll always be your friend." The way to heal the hurting heart is the way of friendship.

The third medication that one has to take is the powerful medicine of prayer. The psalmist says: "The Lord is close to the brokenhearted." And the Lord says: "Come to me all you who are weary and find life burdensome and I will refresh you. For I am meek and humble of heart."

The Lord stands at the door of your heart. He wants to come into the darkness and bring light. He wants to come into the loneliness and bring a feeling of closeness with Him. He wants to come into the cold and bring warmth. He wants to come into the fear and bring hope.

Of course, there are all kinds of quick fixes that suggest themselves: drugs, sex, violence toward self or others. When we hurt so badly, we are very vulnerable. That's why when your heart is hurting, your head has to click in with good problem solving.

Remember: "Friendship divides our grief and doubles our joy." There is something for the pain!

REFLECTION QUESTIONS

Directions: After reading Chapter 3, answer the following questions.

1. Name and explain the three "medications" for emotional hurt.

2. In times of hurt, what does the Good Lord want to give you?

3. Explain the saying "Friendship divides our grief and doubles our joy."

CHAPTER 4

'He Slaps Me Around Because He Loves Me'

The *Brown University Child and Adolescent Behavior Letter* reported in a recent study that almost one-third of sixty-six high school students surveyed interpreted violence as love. Various studies have found that between twelve percent and thirty-five percent of teenagers report experiencing abuse ranging from pushing and shoving to hitting in dating relationships.

We asked our Girls and Boys Town youth about violence and love. They thought about this and we share their comments with you in the hopes that if you or a friend are in an abusive relationship that you will get out of it.

1. "Girls who are in abusive relationships believe guys hit them because they love them. They are just scared to get out because they don't believe anyone else could love them."

2. "Teenage girls don't necessarily feel violence is love. But the things the abuser says tends to convince them."

3. "I'm sure lots of teens interpret violence as love. Otherwise, there wouldn't be girls staying with men who abuse them. A punch in the face doesn't mean 'I love you.'"

4. "When a boyfriend beats his girlfriend, she may think, 'Wow. He must love me very much if he gets this angry when I threaten to leave.'"

5. "When boys tell you they love you and then they beat you, you might think, 'Hey, he loves me and that's why he is beating me.'"

6. "Some girls will say, 'I deserved it when he hit me. I should not have made him mad.' The victim is being blamed. He needs to control his temper."

7. "Some teens have been raised in violent homes and love was shown to them through abuse and violence. So when they get into relationships they think violence is part of showing love."

8. "Some teens feel if a boy beats her, he loves her. Also, the guy thinks if she screams and howls, she loves him."

9. "Maybe if they experienced real love at home, girls might be more receptive to knowing the difference."

10. "Girls need to see that men beat women as a way to control them, not as a measure of how much the guy cares for her."

11. "Some people think that if he loves me, he will fight for me or over me and he will be over-protective."

12. "A violent person tries to make life miserable. He tries to have power over the other person. Real love is where you love others with respect and you don't violate their boundaries."

13. "A lot of times a man has to feel in control. So he tends to try to control the other person even through abuse."

14. "A lot of teen boys use violence as a way to show that they are 'just trying to help me get better.'"

15. "If they hurt you in any way, it isn't love. Love comes from the heart – not from the hand."

16. "Yes, teens today see love and violence going hand in hand. For example, how many times have you heard a girl say: 'He hit me on the arm today, so he must like me.'"

17. "Sometimes girls seem to think that when a guy is mean or abusive toward her, he really loves her that much more."

18. "Some girls feel that it is a boy's way of showing affection."

REFLECTION QUESTIONS

Directions: After reading Chapter 4, answer the following questions.

1. Do you agree that many teens today interpret violence as love? Explain.

2. What do you think would most help teens realize the difference between violence and love? Explain.

3. Choose one of the teen comments in this chapter and write a response to it.

CHAPTER

'I Will Never Love Again'

Many young people are very disappointed in love. The person they care about betrays them or abandons them or just sets them aside.

A spontaneous reaction to disappointment in love is to say that: "I will never love again. I have been hurt too badly. I do not want to even take the risk of that kind of hurt and pain again. Love is a marvelous experience, but it is too hard to obtain, so I will give up on it altogether."

The remedy for mistakes in loving is not to give up on loving, it is to develop better controls over loving. The remedy for mistakes in loving is not to doom oneself to a life of sadness, disappointment, and a lack of joy.

When we are disappointed in love, we simply need to develop a better way to decide where to put our love.

Shall we invest our love and energy in someone who is ready for a commitment or someone who is not ready?

Shall we invest our love in someone who is a friend or someone who is not a friend?

Shall we invest our love in someone who is faithful or someone who is not faithful? Reliable or unreliable?

These are the controls over loving that we need to look at.

If I buy a used car from a particular salesman and he tells me it is terrific, but it turns out to be a "junker," I know the remedy isn't to quit buying cars. The remedy is not to go to such an untrustworthy person again.

Yes, there is something to learn from getting hurt, from being disappointed in love.

The remedy is not to give up on loving. Love is too precious a gift from God. There is another way to develop better controls over loving. The remedy is to learn from our mistakes and not make them again. All of us need to do that.

All of us need to remember that when our emotions have been hurt so badly, we need to turn to the Lord. "The Lord is close to the brokenhearted. He binds up all of their wounds."

Every saint has experienced the Lord mending and bringing healing to the brokenhearted. You can do it too. You can have the same experience. Ask the Lord to come into your life.

REFLECTION QUESTIONS

Directions: After reading Chapter 5, answer the following questions.

1. What is the remedy for mistakes in loving?

2. List five questions mentioned in this chapter that you should ask yourself about whom to love?

3. Why is it wrong to give up on loving after you've been hurt?

CHAPTER

Can You Force Love?

You can teach a dog to sit up and beg or to chase a ball and bring it back. You can teach a cat how to play with a ball of string.

But if you have a crush on someone, can you teach him or her to love you? Can you trick her into loving you? Can you force him to do so?

To have a crush on someone is to believe that he or she is good for you in some way. It is to believe that only that person will make your life happy. It is to believe that you will be important or fulfilled by that person's response.

Can you really manipulate him or her into loving you? Not really. You are basing your hopes on your sexual attraction for the other, your new desire, and a lot of fantasy. None of these will make your dream come true. Throwing yourself at him or her will make things worse, not better.

The root of the problem here is a kind of selfishness. "What I want, I want, and I want it right now. I will do anything to get it." The problem with this behavior is that you not only do not get what you want, but you also get hurt badly.

It is better to learn the lesson of selfishness than to learn the lesson of dependency. To learn the lesson of selfishness, you need to learn that you can't have everything you want. You need to learn that the basis for all love is friendship. You need to learn friendship skills. You will need to learn how to have fun being a friend.

If you throw yourself at the person, you will end up in dependency. If he or she accepts you at all, it will be on that person's terms. He or she will tell you what to do and when to do it and how to do it. You won't feel very good at all. You will feel used and confused.

"If I let my emotions control my thinking and behavior, then when I am angry I will beat up people."

"When I want things in the store, I will take them without paying for them."

"When I feel embarrassed, I will lie and cheat."

"When I feel a sexual attraction, I will say: 'Whatever is meant to be will be.'"

These are all cases of emotions controlling thinking and behavior. That is never a good idea.

Build your life on friendship. It is a solid foundation and a source of enormous happiness.

REFLECTION QUESTIONS

**Directions: After reading Chapter 6, answer the
following questions.**

1. What is the lesson that can be learned from selfishness?

2. Why is it wrong to let your emotions control your
   thinking and behaving?

3. Why doesn't it work when you try to force love?

4. Explain what happens in a relationship if you throw
   yourself at the other person?

5. What should you build your life on? Why?

CHAPTER 7

'You Just Have to Trust Me'

"Baby, you just have to trust me." How often have you heard those words either spoken to yourself or to others?

To understand the meaning of trust, just check out your own experience. Think of when you were a newborn baby. How did you learn to have trust in your mother?

First, when you cried, she would come. That is called reliability. Your mom was reliable, and you knew it. She was so reliable that even if every once in a while she didn't show up, you knew that there must be a reason for that.

Notice also that when your mom showed up, she "brought the goodies." When you cried, your mom came and she gave you what you needed. You often cried because you were hungry. She gave you something to eat. You often cried because your wet pants made you uncomfortable. She changed your diapers.

"Bringing the goodies" is often called commitment. You trusted your mom because she was not only reliable, she was committed. You trusted your mom because she not only came when you cried, she did something to stop your crying.

Those two elements, reliability and commitment, are the same two elements of trust all throughout our lives. When a person says: "Baby, you just have to trust me," you should say to yourself:

- Is he or she reliable? Reliability doesn't mean just does he come when I cry, but can I count on him when he says he will be here at 7:30? Does he show up at 7:30? When she says that she will always be there for me, is she? Or does she make lots of excuses?

- Secondly, is he or she committed? In other words, does he or she bring what is needed? If he says that he will show up at 7:30 with two tickets to a concert and then he shows up without the tickets, he may be reliable, but he is not committed. If she makes lots of excuses about forgetting or being busy, that is a good sign that you shouldn't trust her.

If someone says that he or she will do better tomorrow, wait and see if that happens does. I know a girl whose boyfriend would regularly lose his temper and hit her if she did not do what he wanted. He kept saying that he would completely change and that she would have to trust him, but he never did. She would be very unwise to put any trust in his statements.

After all, words are cheap. Deeds are dear. If there is a discrepancy between words and deeds, the deeds tell the truth. If I say I will respect you and then I make fun of you or deceive you, by my behavior, the truth of the matter is I am not respecting you.

What are the two main characteristics of God, our Heavenly Father? One is reliability. When you cry, He comes. You can always count on Him. When you call on Him, He is near. He will never fail you in that regard.

"Even though I walk in the Valley of Darkness, I will fear no evil. Your rod and your staff, they give me comfort."

Secondly, God is not only reliable, He is committed. He brings what you need. He brings the healing, the hope, the peace, and the joy, if you only open your heart to receive Him and invite Him in.

"The Lord is close to the brokenhearted and He binds up all their wounds."

So what is the answer to: "Baby, you just have to trust me"? The answer is: "I trust people who are worthy of trust, people who are reliable and committed."

REFLECTION QUESTIONS

Directions: After reading Chapter 7, answer the following questions.

1. What are the two elements that demonstrate trustworthiness?

2. What two questions should you ask yourself when someone says to you, "Baby, you just have to trust me"?

3. Explain this phrase: "Deeds tell the truth."

4. Name some ways you can show that you are a reliable and committed friend.

CHAPTER

8

Why Sexual Behavior Is Wrong for Teens

A lot of sexual behavior among teenagers stems from "giving in" and "giving up." If you think there's nothing you can do, you tend to give in. If you simply lament your fate, you give up. Let's look at some examples:

1. Giving In: The road to being accepted. This is a combination of inadequacy and peer pressure. I feel I need to be accepted. I could develop friendship skills but that takes time. Instant access is to follow peer pressure and to engage in sexual behavior.

2. Giving In: Many boys believe that if they date a girl for six months or so they have a right to demand sexual intercourse. To keep a boyfriend, a girl gives in. Of course, if she does, she uses all kinds of rationalizations as all of us do when we give in to things we know we do not want to do.

3. Giving Up: Giving up the high road and not working on friendship skills and chastity is common. There are so many bad role models, and many teens just give up the struggle.

4. Lamenting Fate: The biggest temptation of people who see themselves as victims is to lament their fate. Lamenting your fate is the opposite of honoring the struggle. Lamenting your fate means willingly participating in being the victim and making it seem like "everything's all right."

5. "Let's Pretend": In our adolescent years we want so much to be loved, to be cared for, to be genuine, to be authentic, to be accepted. And being inexperienced, we go out looking for love. And of course our dreams and hopes lead us to see it where it does not yet exist. The desire to fall in love gives birth to infatuation, glowing fantasies, and these, of course, give birth to self-deception. We do not want to miss the chance for love. So we take high risks and lose often. And like a gambler, that makes us take further high risks to make up for our losses.

Giving in to sexual behavior impedes the developmental progress. It harms our grades, harms our relationship with our parents, harms our relationship with our brothers and sisters, harms our learning in almost every facet of adolescence.

Giving in also harms spiritual growth. Whatever impedes union with God and union with others harms spiritual growth.

Giving in to sexual behavior is an example of this. We're now in rebellion. We're now fighting authority, not just in the developmental sense, but in a pathological sense. We are embracing evil on more than one front.

REFLECTION QUESTIONS

Directions: After reading Chapter 8, answer the following questions.

1. Explain why "giving in" to sex is wrong.

2. Explain why "giving up" is wrong.

3. What is "lamenting my fate?"

4. Explain why "let's pretend" is a harmful reason for sexual acting out.

CHAPTER

9

How to Make Dating Healthy and Fun

When a group of boys get together and have good, healthy fun, you notice certain characteristics right away:

- They do things they all enjoy.

- It may be baseball, basketball, or football.

- They talk about things they all enjoy talking about.

- No one in the group is excluded.

- They laugh a lot about silly things and share interesting stories.

- And when they make fun of each other, it's done in a way that keeps them friends.

When girls get together to have a good, healthy fun, there are certain charactcristics:

- They do things they all enjoy.

- It may be sports or a movie or shopping or just visiting.

- No one in the group is excluded.

- They laugh a lot about silly things and share interesting stories.

- And when they make fun of each other, it's done in a way that keeps them friends.

Of course, in any group, there may be one who "causes trouble" for the group. But individuals in the group learn to either help one another or leave.

There's a lot of lessons you can learn in both of these examples when you start dating. Dating can be healthy and fun if you follow that pattern. Let's talk about it:

1. When you start dating, take your time to get to know the other person. Dating gives you a chance to get to know each other slowly. The better you get to know the other person, the more healthy and fun the dating can be.

   - Do things you both like.

   - Don't let the other person always tell you what "we're going to do."

   - If it's one-sided, it won't be that much fun.

   - Insist on both choosing or taking turns choosing what you want to do.

   - If you can't agree on something to do, how can you have any fun?

2. Conversation skills are important.

   - Share interests you have in common.

   - If one person doesn't say anything at all, what fun is there in that?

   - If one person talks so much the other can't get a word in edgewise, what fun is there in that?

   - A one-way relationship is best left behind.

3. Give feedback to each other.

   - This is not easy to do.

   - Most of us want to be liked.

   - And we think we will be liked if we give no feedback.

   - That is not true.

   - If we don't give feedback, we will more likely be used.

   - And we don't want that to happen.

   - Practice giving feedback.

   - It's even a good idea to talk about it with a date.

   - "Joe, I'm the kind of girl who likes to let you know when things are appropriate or inappropriate. Putting me down like you are doing now is inappropriate."

- That's good feedback.
- Joe has to learn to say, "Thanks, Jean. I appreciate you letting me know. I'll try not to do it again. It's more fun when we're both happy."
- That's a great response to feedback.

4. Know what to do if your date wants the relationship quickly to become physical.

- A good dating relationship doesn't mean agreeing on everything.
- It does mean working out differences in a fair way.
- But there are some things which you do not want to compromise on and should not compromise on.
- One is violence. Another is sex.
- Set boundaries quickly.
- Don't tolerate ever, ever, ever being hit.
- Don't tolerate pressure tactics to have sex for the other's physical gain.
- If the other person starts threatening or begging or pleading or making fun of you, that's not fun and that's not healthy.
- Tell him or her to stop doing so or the dating stops.
- And if it continues, then that means that caring and sharing are not what that person intends for you.

5. There are some good basic rules for healthy dating:

- Don't let yourself be used by another. Why? Because you can't have fun or be healthy if you are being used.

- Take your time. Why? Because otherwise you will trust too much, too soon, and that's not fun or healthy.

- Ask yourself if you are treated fairly. Why? Because you can't have fun and be healthy if the other person pushes you around or always gets his or her way.

- If you are being used, ask for help in breaking off the relationship. Why? Because it's no fun and you'll need help.

- Don't lose respect for yourself. Why? It's not fun and not healthy. If you have lost respect for yourself, ask for help to regain it.

- Learn from the mistakes of others. Why? Because you won't live long enough to make all the mistakes yourself.

Dating is meant to be fun and healthy. Enjoy.

REFLECTION QUESTIONS

Directions: After reading Chapter 9, answer the following questions.

1. Name five ways dating can be healthy and fun.

2. According to this chapter, what is the purpose of dating?

3. Why are conversation skills important for dating?

4. What are the six rules of dating?

5. Which two rules will help you the most? Why?

CHAPTER

10

Promises, Promises

If an employer promises to pay you $5 an hour and in your first paycheck you only get paid $4.50 an hour, that's a big disappointment. The employer broke his promise, and he broke the law. It hurts you. And there's something you can do about it.

When an employer breaks a contract with an employee and pays less than was agreed to, you need to explain to the employer that you will take this matter to a law enforcement agency. The United States Department of Labor has an office in your town. It's a good place to start. If the place of employment has a union, you need to go to the union steward. You will be upset. You will be angry. You might even want to do something destructive, something stupid. But common sense tells you not to do that. Thank goodness.

When someone breaks your heart, however, you are not just angry. You are deeply hurt. And the Department of Labor can't help you.

If someone in a dating relationship promises to be there for you, to care for you, and does just the opposite, that's not just a big disappointment to you. It's a disaster. It hurts and it breaks your heart. That person didn't break the law, he or she broke a promise. There's a big difference, and there's something you should do about it.

Think about a girl and boy who have been in a healthy relationship for a long time but now the boy cheats on her. She loves him so much it scares her. Think of all the trust, faith, hope, love, honesty, and respect she had before he hurt her. This hurt causes great unhappiness and can lead to never opening up and trusting again.

The hurting and the anger come from a broken heart. And you are often tempted to do very foolish, very hurtful things. Too bad that with the loss of the relationship comes a momentary loss of common sense.

You may really want the relationship to continue because you have invested so much of yourself in it. So, you may try to make the other person want to stay with you.

That gets you in a real bind, because the more you try to make them stay with you, the more you have to sacrifice the loving, caring, sharing relationship you have cherished so much. The more you want to make him or her stay with you, the more you will have to sacrifice in a bad way. You will have to do what the other person wants when and how he or she wants you to do it. You will have to meet the other person's needs and forget about your own. You will have to sacrifice your self-worth. You will have to sacrifice your self-respect. But by doing that, you will be disrespected by the other person even more.

You can do something about broken promises, however, something helpful, healthful, and hopeful.

A person who has been hurt as you have needs to share these feelings. This is true. You need to share these feelings with someone who cares, someone who listens, someone you can trust. There is an old saying: "Friendship doubles our joy and divides our grief." That's true. If you share your suffering, hurt, and sorrow with someone else, the other person can carry part of your burden. That's a good feeling.

Secondly, examine that desire to make him or her want to stay with you and do some problem solving with it. If you talk him or her into staying with you, the other person will end up tricking and manipulating you. How will he or she feel about becoming a person like that? How will friends feel about that person?

More importantly, it won't bring you what you really want, which is the old relationship the way it was before. Now you will have to settle for somehow or other relating to the person in a fragmented way. In a way that is hurtful to you.

Sometimes good problem-solving skills will suggest that the relationship is "beyond repair." You shouldn't want to stay in a relationship where you lose your self-respect, are hurt deeply, or arc treated with disrespect. You don't want to stay in a relationship that is hurtful.

Sometimes in a relationship you can identify the problem but are too caught up in the routine of it. Once you have been doing something for so long, it almost feels wrong to do it another way. And a lot of people feel obligated to do or say what the other wants to hear.

The first step out of the relationship is to talk with someone who can help you realize that the remedy for mistaken loving is not to give up trying to love, but to move forward and develop healthy relationships.

It is a great time to keep yourself close to the Lord. He will never reject you, but will rather hold you close in the palm of His hand. The Lord will tell you how much you as a person are beautiful and loved. As the Psalmist says: "The Lord is close to the brokenhearted and heals all their wounds."

And remember how important it is to have respect for yourself and be able to be strong before you depend on a boyfriend or girlfriend to cover your insecure feelings.

REFLECTION QUESTIONS

Directions: After reading Chapter 10, answer the following questions.

1. What are some healthful and hopeful things that can be done about broken promises in relationships?

2. Why is it important to talk to someone about how you are feeling and thinking?

3. How can staying close to God help?

How Could This Happen to Me?

"How could this happen to me?"

Maybe it's just a string of bad luck. The transmission in my girlfriend's car burned up because she forgot to put oil in. The phone company cut off my service because I didn't pay my bill for two months. My school wouldn't let me take my final exam because of overdue library books. When I returned the books, I took the test and still flunked it. My mom has Crohn's disease, stopped taking her medication, and was rushed to the emergency room. My life is surrounded by troubles.

Why do bad things like this happen to good people like me? Is it because I am having a lot of bad luck? Or because God does not care about me? Or because I freely choose to do bad and now have to face the consequences?

Your girlfriend freely chose to neglect regular engine maintenance. She was free to do so, but she was not free from the consequences of that choice – burning out her transmission. A student is free to neglect his overdue books at the library, but he cannot control the consequences of that free choice – being barred from an examination. You are free to neglect studying. However, then you have no choice but to accept the consequences of that free choice – an "F" on the final exam.

When your transmission goes out or you flunk a final exam, you are tempted to deaden the pain with short-term solutions. You can freely choose to do drugs or alcohol, deadening the pain for a time. However, you are not free from the consequences of that choice, namely, feeling even worse after the high or the hangover.

So the old warning rings true: "If you can't do the time, don't do the crime." If you don't want your transmission to burn out, you can freely choose regular maintenance. If you can't stand getting an "F," then don't freely choose to neglect your studies. Choose wisely to study well.

Of course, you can always blame the consequences on somebody else. Your girlfriend can say it was the manufacturer's fault for making such a bad transmission. You can say it was the librarian's fault for making such a dumb rule. But we all know those are cop-outs.

The best thing we can do is to feel good about ourselves by using behavior with good consequences.

Bill, age 16, chose to drink so much that by graduation from high school he was a full-blown alcoholic. He was free to choose to drink, but he was not free to escape the consequences of alcoholism. The best thing he can do now is to freely choose to go to AA and freely choose to work the AA program to enjoy the good consequences of sobriety. Through our choices, we create our own identity. If I freely choose to steal repeatedly, I have freely chosen the consequences, namely, I am now a thief.

Choices determine our future. Wise choices bring a happy future and the beginning of wisdom is found in those wise choices.

So a lot of what happens to us that is bad we could have simply avoided by doing good. If we freely choose to do bad, the consequences will be very unpleasant for us. But if we freely choose to do good, the consequences will be more pleasant for us.

REFLECTION QUESTIONS

Directions: After reading Chapter 11, answer the following questions.

1. In your opinion, why do bad things happen to good people?

2. What is the connection between freedom and responsibility?

3. What could you do to avoid some of the bad things that happen?

Credits

Production: Mary Steiner
Layout: Anne Hughes
Cover Design: Margie Brabec
009-19-0057